# Preaching

# Unchurched

## in an Entertainment Culture

### Roger Standing

Regional Minister/Team Leader
Southern Counties Baptist Association

**GROVE BOOKS LIMITED**
RIDLEY HALL RD  CAMBRIDGE  CB3 9HU

# Contents

**The Cover Illustration** is by Peter Ashton

**First Impression** May 2002
**ISSN** 1367-0840
**ISBN** 1 85174 498 3

# Introduction

## 1

*The thumping music from the disco stopped and the lights in the church hall were switched on.*

Several hundred teenagers dutifully sat down on the floor or on the chairs pushed hard up against the walls. The DJ left the anonymity provided by banks of lights, speakers and twin-deck console and began to talk about Jesus and the ultimate questions of life.

Well, that was the late 70s and I was only just beyond being a teenager myself. Working as an evangelist based at Central Hall in Liverpool, we were keen to explore new ways of reaching the new generation for Christ. A few years earlier I had passed over the opportunity of professional employment as a DJ after coming to faith myself. God seemed to be changing the direction of my life. In Liverpool it just seemed the natural thing to do to bring together my work as a DJ and evangelism in the 'Jesus Disco.' Over a period of two years we saw hundreds of young people commit to following Jesus and link up with their local church.

Times move on. Still committed to exploring new and creative initiatives in evangelism, by the late 1990s I was the Senior Minister at West Croydon Baptist Church in South London. My colleague Joe Davis was always bubbling with new ideas and suggested that we try something very different that might appeal to the unchurched friends and relations of our congregation. Having a broadly Willow Creek model in mind and with six months of advertising at the local Warner Village in place, our *First Tuesday/First Sunday* project was born.

*Good numbers attended the monthly events, and the church loved it*

The night we sat in the cinema at Valley Park, Croydon, watching our advertisement flick onto the big screen every few minutes while beginning to consume a gigantic bucket of popcorn and ridiculously large Fanta, I knew we were doing something very different and extremely exciting. The fact that a newly released Bond movie was to follow was the icing on the cake.

Joe coined the term 'Christertainment' to cover our blend of pure entertainment themed alongside a gospel presentation with accompanying TV and movie clips, pop videos and the obligatory PowerPoint presentation. It was great. Good numbers attended the monthly events, the church loved it and it was one of the most exciting and rewarding projects I have ever been involved with. But how well did it work? How significant are initiatives like this? On what basis do we attempt them, both biblically and theologically? While undertaking further study at Denver Seminary in Colorado I had the opportunity to explore more deeply the received wisdom behind such evangelistic endeavours. Received wisdom can be quite clear that seeking to make the proclamation of the gospel more relevant to contemporary culture is both scripturally warranted and practically effective. This booklet tells the story of what we did, why we did it and what we learned.

# 2
## What on Earth is Christertainment?

*I was left staring like a rabbit caught in the headlights of an on-coming car!*

There was an impending sense of doom alongside a mild sense of euphoria. It had all seemed pretty good in the planning stage, but was it about to go horribly wrong? On one hand we had a TV crew at church who, having interviewed three or four people, were now setting up to record the whole of our monthly, midweek alternative service, *First Tuesday*. But on the other, the local press had caught on and run a *'Church recruits sexy babes to attract the faithful!'* feature that had not cast us in a good light. The advertising hoarding outside the church on our busy junction had been proclaiming, 'Great SEXpectations' for the previous two weeks, and, by the look of the assembled audience, it had done its work. Now, as I walked back into the church I contemplated how *London Today* would report the event the following day— would it be acclaim or ridicule?

It was great. Our PA sound went down at the beginning of the talk, the computer froze out an audio file at an embarrassingly inappropriate moment and one of the video clips was really badly miscued. I wondered why this night, of all nights? We all waited with baited breath the following lunchtime to see what *London Today* had made of it. We were not on! Thinking that we had been bumped for a major news item we rang in to find out what had happened. Their explanation was reassuring—they got their lighting levels all wrong and none of their material was usable! Perhaps it was just as well.

## The Vision

Our *First Tuesday/First Sunday* project had begun as the vision of my co-worker, Joe Davis. Having responsibility for our outreach ministry and a passion for the seeker-sensitive approach, Joe had wanted to put together an entertaining, high-quality, cringe-free event that would be attractive to the unchurched. We were already committed to an evangelism strategy based on Laurence Singlehurst's, *Sowing, Reaping, Keeping,* and this initiative fitted the 'Sowing 2' category.[1] We wanted it to be the means of communicating the insight and wisdom of God's heart for His world. As such it would easily dovetail into the church's overall vision of where we sensed the Lord was leading us.

> *We wanted it to be the means of communicating the insight and wisdom of God's heart for His world*

Our planning had given shape to the vision. Running the programme midweek would minimize the 'church service' perceptions in the minds of potential attendees, and running it in our blacked-out sanctuary, under spotlights would help foster an environment of theatre-cum-cinema which was the model we were working with. Our target audience was 20–30-somethings, so we planned an 8pm start for a 60–75 minute show. And 'show' is the right word. There were to be no worship songs, no organ, no pulpit, no offering, none of the normal components of a Christian service. Rather, the programme centred on wholesome entertainment, sometimes with an implicitly Christian flavour, most often not. The varied diet of live music, performance poetry, dance routines, escapology, stage magic and drama all went to set up the talk presentation, which was my responsibility. Thus the concept of 'Christertainment' was born.

We booked crossover Christian band *Last Exit* because of their ability to perform appropriate secular music on our chosen themes, and so we planned the launch. There was no doubt that it was an ambitious undertaking, and we were not a mega-church with abundant resources to hand. West Croydon Baptist Church is a multi-cultural congregation of around 200 members, with a Victorian, three-quarter gallery preaching house located in the middle of a road traffic island towards the centre of the London Borough of Croydon. We had little in the way of financial reserves and, each year, just seemed to cover our budget and expenses. Most of the congregation were not professional people, though just over half were under 45.

Central to the whole concept was the use of a video/data projector, but that is an expensive piece of kit. Yet one afternoon in the run up to our first events, one of our most enthusiastic supporters of evangelism asked as she lay dying of cancer what would be a significant thing to purchase to help our outreach. She wanted to make it happen before she died. Now an 8'x10' screen sits in the upper pulpit area where the rail has been removed, with back projection from above the organist's seat.

Then, some bright spark had the idea of advertising in the local Warner Village Multiplex. Well, Valley Park had just opened and they were short of advertising. They offered us a still slide for 8 seconds, 8 times before every movie on all 8 screens for 6 months at a discounted cost of £2000. Our budget would not stand it, but a one-off appeal raised the money, to the pound, on one Sunday morning three weeks before Christmas 1997.

*Our goal was to grab people's eyes and ears and fully engage them*

Part of our overall goal, alongside the use of video clips, was to include computer graphics and audio files during both the programme and the talk. We wanted to grab people's eyes and ears and fully engage them. To do that you need someone who knows what they are doing. The Lord sent us a computer expert, who was both theologically trained and had some experience in exactly what were hoping to begin to explore.

## Appraisal

Thirteen months and eleven presentations later we entered a period of appraisal. Attendance had ranged from 80–150 and we could not actually identify quite a large number of those who came because we just did not know who they were. A few had started attending on a Sunday, and a smaller number have since been baptized and would say that *First Tuesday* was one of the influences the Lord used on their spiritual journey to faith. But then, in seeing it as a 'Sowing 2' event (in Singlehurst's terms) we did not make explicit calls for commitment with accompanying invitations to come to the front for prayer.

*We had misjudge our target audier very badly indeec*

We received lots of affirmation from people, and it seemed as though the wider church loved the fact that we were doing it, even if they were not coming themselves, recognizing that it was just not their thing. However, we discovered that we had misjudged our target audience very badly indeed. Tuesday nights were not a good time at all. For a start, for those in work 8pm midweek was a turn-off. By the time they had got home and eaten it was not so easy to get out. Plus, if they had had a bad day the temptation to stay home was overwhelming. And our wider network of contacts in the target group had a large number of single parent families. While some did make it, the need to organize baby-sitting was a major issue and a significant disincentive to coming.

So we began to talk and reflect on what we had discovered on timing and ultimately came up with the ideal alternative—Sunday morning. Listening to what we were being told meant the surprise of discovering that we did not have to be as radically different and 'alternative' as we had supposed.

*We did not have to be as radically different and 'alternative' as we had supposed*

We were amazed and thrilled when the church members unanimously agreed to trial *First Sunday* for a year during 2000. By Singlehurst's definitions we changed the event from a 'Sowing 2' activity to a 'Reaping' event. We also included a modest amount of worship. Initially we had thought about moving to two services on these Sunday mornings, but the leaders were adamant that this was an initiative for the whole church to participate in and own, and for it to be otherwise would be to needlessly allow a potential for divisiveness. Our big millennium initiative was therefore the launch of *First Sunday*. On Boxing Day 1999 a new hoarding was erected, advertising the event: *'Tomorrow began yesterday.'*

In the following months we explored 'in your face issues' like racism and religious fanatics alongside love, relationships and a show-stopping 'Simpson's Sunday.' Sunday morning subtlety changed things though. The worship was not easy to pitch well, the entertainment did not sit so easily in our normal Sunday Service slot and we found ourselves becoming less adventurous and more conservative as we explored the issues in front of us. That said, the events were well received, people who did not normally come to church came and a few made a commitment to follow Jesus.

# 3

## Does It Stand Up to Scrutiny?

*Do we really need to consider doing things differently? Are not the tried and tested ways best anyhow?*

The human heart does not change and neither does the Bible, so what is the problem? The fact is, the world has changed.

## The World Has Changed

The decline in attendance at worship services in the UK has been dramatic. A 13% decline in the ten-year period 1979–89 had accelerated to 22% in the nine years 1989–98. Indeed, the number of under-15s in contact with the church has fallen from 25% to 19%, while only 5% of twenty-somethings attend worship in England.[2] The rapidity of this fall has led many to ask serious questions regarding its causes and how it can be reversed.

On one hand, many hold the nostalgic belief that, if they only pray, wait faithfully, and remain true to the tradition they received, the Lord will make tomorrow like yesterday and the 'good old days' they remember. Others, recognizing that the world at the beginning of the twenty-first century is a vastly different place from that of a century ago, look for fundamental change to address the new cultural context in which we live.

Here I seek to address one facet of changing Western culture and the impact it has on evangelistic preaching. It is the issue of effective communication in an information-saturated and multimedia-enhanced culture. The present generation of forty-somethings were weaned on television; those under forty continue to have increasingly sophisticated tastes as they consume electronic media through terrestrial, cable and digital TV, videos, CDs, DVDs, CDROMs and the Internet. It is hardly surprising therefore that the 'It was boring' critique of many a teenager after a church service was overwhelmingly substantiated in a survey conducted by Gallup in the United Kingdom. They found that the clear majority in every age group under fifty found traditional church worship services boring. From Monday to Saturday we live in a world shaped by TV; failure to engage with the implications of this prevailing culture has serious consequences for our communication of the gospel. We may be literally 'boring people to hell.'

*We may be literally 'boring people to hell'*

Neil Postman, in his acclaimed commentary *Amusing Ourselves to Death*, outlines the reason for the boredom in his analysis of public debate in contemporary society.[3] He charts how the 'age of exposition' has given way to the 'age of show business,' as the all-pervasive growth of TV has displaced the role of the printing press in public discourse on politics, education, and religion. Consequently public discourse, he says, 'has become shrivelled and absurd.' With TV as the command centre of the new epistemology (theory of knowledge), all public understanding is coloured by its biases and must be communicated according to the new supra-ideology of entertainment.

This is clearly seen in the first two post-war generation groups, the Baby Boomers and Generation X. Television has been central to the experience of Boomers, the first generation to have grown up with it. It provided for them a unifying common experience that introduced the adult world at a very early age. Its impact has been profound, replacing word with image in communication, and delivering a culture typified by instancy and immediacy. Seeing, not reading, is the Boomers' basis for believing. In addition they are '...deeply enmeshed in the narrative tradition—for at heart they are storytellers, and like all storytellers, they know that life is an open-ended plot.'[4]

## The Information Age

'Xers' are the first wave of humanity to reach adulthood on the post-industrial side of the historical divide, and this has dramatic implications for them. Pre-eminent among these developments is the arrival of the 'information age.' The average Xer teenager spends two to three hours a day watching TV and will consume eighty-nine movies in a year. Significantly, 38% spend around a quarter of their TV time watching the cable channel MTV. This is important because MTV is a significant contributor to the shaping of the reduced attention span and decrease in the boredom threshold among teenagers. MTV videos have edit cuts on average every three seconds and MTV commercials are even faster paced. In addition, figures for the early 1990s indicate a daily session for Xers of 30–40 minutes on a personal computer (PC). With the proliferation of PCs and increasing access to the Internet, it is fair to estimate that this is now a very conservative figure.

*MTV videos have edit cuts on average every three seconds*

Electronic media are destined to become ever more sophisticated and of increasing quality, with an explosion of variety and range of available product options. Third millennial films will be dominated by computer-generated virtual sequences. Multimedia-rich presentations will be routine in the business world. Professional presentations, already replete with computer driven graphics, sound, video and video conferencing, will increasingly be judged not just by content but by the way the technology itself is used.

Third millennial TV will not be exempt from radical change either. Audience scoping will provide instant analysis of how viewers are feeling, and interactive TV will replace patterns of passive viewing with participation in program content and delivery. The 500 channels soon to be available through digital broadcast techniques will be supplanted by the total choice of Internet TV and the spawning of special interest channels. As technology improves it will provide instant access to 100,000 films starting right now at the push of a button or 300,000 popular programmes after a delay of less than 20 seconds, all of digital TV quality. In addition, virtual reality technology is rapidly improving, becoming cheaper and more user friendly.

## The Style of Communication Has Changed

It has been estimated that people between the ages of 25–40 have watched an average of 30–40,000 hours of TV and some 250,000 advertisements. This has altered the mental skills and listening aptitudes of society because it requires less concentration and effort and is more entertaining. More than this, it can be argued that TV, videos, and movies engage both the rational and emotional dimensions of the viewers' consciousness. The preacher's audience is very different from what it was a few decades ago. People listen and process information differently. The staple diet of the electronic media is story. It is found in the daily ration of soap opera, the movie blockbuster, the mini-narratives of commercials, or the 'stories' in the nightly news. To preach in the same way as previous generations will be as effective a method of communication as a jerky old black-and-white silent movie in a state of the art movie theatre with wide screen and Dolby Surround Sound.

The practical impact of TV on audiences has been widely charted and in relation to traditional preaching the consequences are significant. TV is commonly acknowledged to:

- convey pictures rather than concepts.
- convey information in bites or impressions, rather than sequentially.
- combine verbal and non-verbal communication.
- have reduced the concentration span.
- have greatly increased passive listening.

The casual and relaxed mood of TV is significant too, with a more direct appeal to the feelings rather than to thought. As a medium it is intimate but impersonal, with the use of the autocue simulating the eye contact of oral communication while a prepared script is read. By comparison, a worship service with the use of the Bible is a far more serious and formal endeavour. It is hardly surprising that the boredom threshold when listening to a sermon has substantially reduced over the years.

Recognizing that there is a complex relationship between the Holy Spirit, faith, and culture, there would seem to be no doubt that preaching must change and adapt. This is part of Christianity's infinite translatability that always disturbs the orthodox when confronted by a new cultural milieu. It calls for a paradigm shift on the part of the preacher, characterized by a shift from thinking in ideas to thinking in story.

## The Power of Narrative

There is nothing new about storytelling and the power of a narrative to hold an audience. From the oldest civilizations that told community stories around the campfire to our own family stories that are handed down from generation to generation, stories have been important. While they have never gone out of fashion, only recently have they taken on a new ascendancy, an ascendancy born of TV rather than books. In 1996, the average American spent 100 hours reading books against 1,600 watching broadcast and cable TV.

*The common connection is the power of narrative*

Increasingly, people think in images rather than concepts, so stories stick. Stories are also effective tools in creating identification and aiding retention. Many social commentators talk of the 'reoralization' of Western culture. If a literate culture thinks in ideas, an oral culture thinks in stories.

There may be a world of difference between TV viewers whose preference varies from soap operas, to sci-fi adventures, period dramas, documentaries, and news programmes, but the common connection is the power of narrative. Even game shows hook the audience by the same method: who will survive the cull of 'weakest links'? Who will become the millionaire? Who will be the last person left in the 'Big Brother' house?

*The unchurched are more combative, lonelier and less flexible than previous generations*

To become more culturally sensitive some suggest a change in style is inevitable in evangelistic communication. If it is to follow TV, it will need a sharper, snappier pace, often with rapid changes of theme and mood. There is also an increased sophistication in TV producers who create multi-layered programs that are less dependent on linear flow and leave gaps in narrative and argument for the viewer to jump. All of this has implications for the preacher.

Interestingly, recent research conducted by George Barna in the United States confirms that the solitary nature of many contemporary cultural experiences (like watching the TV and surfing the internet) have left the unchurched tending not to be 'people persons.' Barna charts how they are more combative, lonelier and less flexible when compared with previous generations. Consequently they are not especially willing to bend over backwards to fit into a relational style of congregation and are more likely to become attached to special events rather than belonging to groups.[5]

In the light of present and future cultural change churches do not have the luxury of simply perpetuating the forms of the past. To do so would not only miss out on reaching the present generation of non-Christians, but also risk losing the rising generation of Christians. Graham Cray, the Bishop of Maidstone, concurs with these insights in his recent contribution to the Grove Evangelism Series:

> But we now know that *all* Christianity is contextualized, it *is* not culture-free, nor is it *meant* to be. When context changes church has to change to be faithful to an unchanging gospel.[6]

## The Unchanging Word of God

What has the Bible got to say as we consider how to get the Word out into our contemporary Western cultural context? Given that the content of the gospel message does not change, does our methodology matter? Or is it timeless too, making this a merely superficial discussion of style in the light of fashionable changes in communication technology and practice? A closer look reveals that the issues involved actually strike at the core of the relationship between the gospel and culture. This relationship affects every facet of Christianity including the evangelistic task. So, how far is it appropriate that cultural issues of presentational style should affect the proclamation the gospel? My passion has always been to see the gospel contextualized in the contemporary host culture without compromising its content.

*Is this a merely superficial discussion of fashion and style?*

> Jesus said to his disciples, 'As the Father has sent me, I am sending you.'                                                                    John 20.21

The question therefore has to be asked, how did the Father send the Son? Theologically this is seen as involving both incarnation and kenosis.

In the incarnation God's eternal Word and a real man became one at a specific place and time. Those who met Jesus had 'seen' him (John 1.14). He was an historical person. He lived a real life, in the real world, at a specific point in history. Profoundly influenced by Hellenism, Alexander the Great and Rome, Jesus' mother tongue would have been Aramaic. He was also able to read the Jewish Scriptures in Hebrew and, having ministered in the Decapolis (Mark 7.31), it is highly likely that he spoke Greek. In addition there is the probability that he also understood the administrative language of the Roman Empire, Latin. He understood the cosmopolitan life of Galilee and the nature of living in a state that had lost its autonomy to an occupying military power. These influences would have been in sharp relief for him having established Capernaum as the centre for his early ministry (Matthew 4.13). The city was situated on a provincial border, and hosted a customs post with a resident Roman garrison on the Via Maris trade route. His coming, his incarnation, was specific to a particular context—it was contextualized.

Kenosis is the partner of incarnation and relates to what happened within the second person of the Trinity as he took flesh.

> Who, being in very nature God, did not consider equality with God something to be grasped, but made himself nothing...(Phil 2.6–8)

The example of Jesus is not one of sacrificing essential attributes or abilities, but rather one of humility and self-sacrifice that puts the interests of others before himself. Human understanding may reason that God-likeness means having your own way. Christ, however, did not count equality with God as something that could be grasped (literally 'snatched'); on the contrary, he 'made himself nothing.' Christ's sacrifice is all about giving himself in the service of others. He empties himself of the privileges, honour, role and status of his pre-incarnate being by taking on the role of a servant/slave: one who had no rights or privileges except to serve his master.

A third strand is found in the instructions of Jesus in Matthew 28.18–19, 'The Great Commission.' It is to this passage that we have looked for the determining command of Jesus regarding mission and evangelism. The influence of 'The Great Commission' on successive generations of Christians cannot be underestimated. Indeed, many theologians would agree with David Bosch in affirming 'The pivotal nature of these verses.'[7]

*Cultural sensitivity is an integral part of our fidelity to the Great Commission*

The Greek phrase *panta ta ethne* ('all the nations') has great significance. It is most likely that *ethne* is best translated as 'ethnic, tribe, people or culture group' rather the than more usual 'nations' with its implied reference to political states and administrative boundaries. This reading has the benefit of taking culture more seriously. Cultural sensitivity is thus an integral part of our fidelity to the 'Great Commission.'

The preaching of both Jesus and Paul shed further light on this. Preaching was the first priority in Jesus' ministry in Luke 4.43:

> But he said, 'I must preach the good news of the kingdom of God to the other towns also, because that is why I was sent.'

A brief survey of the preaching material he used gives some insight into how culturally tailored his communication was. He spoke about what people knew, and used that as a means to open up the truth of God to his hearers. He employed insights gleaned from agriculture (Matthew 9.35–38, 13.1–43), the countryside (Matthew 5.25–34), the construction industry (Matthew 7.24–29) and familial rites of passage (Matthew 22.1–14). On other occasions he picked up on social prejudices (Luke 10.25–37), social customs (Luke 15.8–10), personal relationships (Luke 15.11–31), the experience of management (Luke 16.1–15) and of casual labour (Matthew 20.1–16).

*Jesus deployed a whole range of preaching styles and strategies*

Jesus was also able to deploy a whole range of preaching styles and strategies as he addressed his listeners. Sometimes he would begin by speaking about their personal experience (Matthew 16.2–3), other times he started with the Scriptures (Matthew 5.21–48). Sometimes he took an interactive approach and answered their questions (Luke 10.25–37), other times he asked poignant questions of them (Matthew 11.7–19).

## Paul's Approach

The considerable lengths to which Jesus went to establish a rapport with his listeners is then echoed in the flexibility of approach Paul used as he moves from Jewish synagogue circles into the pagan Gentile context.

Having preached regularly in the marketplace at Athens, Paul was courteously invited to address a meeting of the Areopagus on Mars Hill. This was a group of thirty men who comprised the most exclusive court in the city. He addressed them in the style and with the modesty with which they would have been familiar. He did not adopt a confrontational attitude that challenged and denounced their idolatry, but chose to come alongside his hearers. He commended them for being 'very religious,' and used their 'altar to an unknown God,' which he had observed in the city, as a

*Paul did not present the fundamentals of his teaching so much as arouse their curiosity*

focus to get their interest and attention. Using the debating technique of *insinuatio*, with which they would also have been familiar, Paul did not present the fundamentals of his teaching so much as attempt to arouse their curiosity.

At one point Paul angles his speech to the pantheism of the Stoics: '...he is not far from each one of us' (v 27b). In doing so he quotes from one of their poets, Aratus, 'We are his offspring' (v 28b). Then, at another point, he utilizes his knowledge of Greek philosophy as he deploys a quote from Epimenides, 'For in him we live and move and have our being' (v 28). He demonstrates that he is quite prepared to use and redeem pagan thought when it contains a glimmering of truth, and in so doing applies what was said of Zeus, the chief god of their pantheon, to Jesus. Paul outlines the simple theory behind this mission strategy in 1 Corinthians 9.19–23.

> To the Jews I became like a Jew, to win the Jews...To the weak I became weak, to win the weak. I have become all things to all people, so that by all possible means I might save some. I do all this for the sake of the gospel, that I may share in its blessings.

Paul is convinced of the requirement to do whatever it takes to communicate the gospel to whomever he is addressing.

## Is This 'Dumbing Down' the Gospel?

So how far can we go with our evangelistic preaching? Can we enhance it with the insights from contemporary communication theory and practice, and still call it preaching? Or is it so wedded to a particular set of methodologies that are integral to it and, without which, it just ceases to be Christian preaching at all and becomes merely an exercise in communication? An elderly Methodist preacher once said to me,

> Roger, there are only two occasions on which you are to preach the gospel—in season and out of season!

If it is always the right time to preach the gospel, the question is whether an inappropriate approach to the task can change the season. It was to this screen-driven, postmodern culture, with its rediscovery of the art of storytelling, that we addressed our *First Tuesday/First Sunday* initiative.

Not everyone is as convinced of the necessity of such an engagement with contemporary culture. There is another view that sees this embracing of the present worldview as a dangerous threat to the content and integrity of the gospel. In the United States this debate has placed those who seek a more culturally-attuned outreach to the unchurched under the critical scrutiny of John MacArthur, David Wells, Os Guinness and others.

To adopt such a contemporary style is obviously to begin to integrate elements of our entertainment culture, or 'age of show business' as Postman puts it, into the life of the church. It is no surprise to discover the controversy that has surrounded Willow Creek Community Church in this regard.

MacArthur has accused them of being 'ashamed of the gospel' in a book of that title,[8] and others have labelled them as being part of the entertainment business. Ed Dobson of Willow Creek has not been slow to reply. Who created the arts? Whose idea was it to communicate the truth through a wide variety of artistic genres? While he acknowledges inherent dangers in a 'visually' oriented approach to church in contrast with a 'listening' approach, he does not think that visual stimuli are wrong *per se*. The role of visual communication is not to replace the spoken word, but to support it, just as the Old Testament prophets often illustrated truth with their actions.

*The role of visual communication is not to replace the spoken word, but to support it*

Interestingly, this is exactly the criticism that is levelled at those who want to engage the gospel with culture by David Wells and Os Guinness. Wells believes that there is an 'anti-theological' mood gripping the evangelical world and changing its configuration. Reality, as a consequence, is accessed through subjective experience rather than through objective thought. The contemporary 'video culture' gives preference to intuition over reason, and to feeling over truth.[9] Guinness is in agreement with Wells and holds that anti-intellectualism is 'both a scandal and a sin' because it is contrary to Jesus' first command to love the Lord our God with all our minds.[10] He sees TV as being a major contributing influence in the 'dumbing down' of contemporary culture into 'idiot culture.'

For Guinness, television has a series of inbuilt biases that are anathema to the gospel. He believes its simplistic thought and intense emotion give TV a bias against understanding and rationality. Rapidity and variety stop viewers from engaging with the consequences of what is experienced, and give the medium a bias against responsibility. The preoccupation with the present results in a bias against memory and history. While credibility is linked with plausibility, giving a bias against truth and accuracy, credibility has more to do in this context with performance than principle. He concludes that we are losing our ability to manage ideas and to think. Hearing and reading are slow, sequential, demanding and analytical processes that put a premium on truth, understanding, and judgment.

*Rapidity and vari[ety] stop viewers from engaging with the consequences*

Visual communication, by contrast, is faster, easier, more immediate, and more intuitive. It moves by association and not analysis. For Guinness a controlling principle is the theological truth that 'In the beginning was the Word.'[11] He is convinced that evangelicalism has uncritically and wholeheartedly bought into modernity and consumerism.[12]

Richard Mouw, however, suggests that Wells and Guinness have passed too quickly over some very important issues. He suggests 'a hermeneutic of charity' to their mindset of suspicion.[13] While Jesus may not have been a crowd pleaser, Mouw remembers that St Augustine observed how Jesus performed miracles to get the attention of the common people.

Mouw considers this disdain for popular religious culture to be a theological defect that fails to develop an adequate theological understanding of ordinary religious people. Popular religion is the expression of men and women who bear God's image. He observes that Jesus approached people in terms of the peculiarities of their context, and that the Incarnation itself is a profound exercise in divine 'tailoring.' He quotes the Bishop of Edinburgh, Richard Holloway, against himself.

> *Disdain for popular religious culture is a theological defect*

> More people go to discos than to high opera, and one of the courageous things about evangelicals is their ability to embrace bad taste for the sake of the gospel.[14]

Mouw is much more taken with the sentiments of Father Patrick Ryan who, commenting on the kitsch of popular Catholic devotion, shared the profound insight that

> Jesus subjected to the humiliation of bad artistic presentation pours himself out even for those with little or no aesthetic sensibility...How often does the Son reveal the Father in tasteless posters and plastic statues that glow in the dark? More often than I once supposed.[15]

# 4

*With the case for seeking to contextualize the proclamation of the gospel for our contemporary, multimedia-rich environment clearly made, how effective were our attempts with the 'First Tuesday/First Sunday' initiative?*

To find out, a research strategy was devised under the guidance of Denver Seminary to answer the question:

> 'Will listeners to the different preaching styles used at West Croydon Baptist Church, London, England, respond differently according to age, church background and Christian commitment?'

The purpose of this piece of research was to move beyond the uncritical presuppositions about 'seeker-oriented' events and seek to find statistical evidence that corroborates the case for change which, in the UK, has remained largely anecdotal and intuitional. While there are many angles that such a study could have taken, we explored two specific issues. The first was to compare responses of the participants according to their age, church background, and Christian commitment, to the two different preaching styles. These were the traditional verse-by-verse expository approach which was the norm at Sunday morning worship services, and the topical format developed in the monthly alternative service. The latter was more inductive in character and also had narrative and conversational qualities.

The second issue explored was the significance of multimedia in the responses to the sermon styles. In the context of the research, multimedia represents the use of computer graphics and audio files alongside the projection of TV and film clips via video while the sermon is being preached. While it is the topical format of *First Tuesday/First Sunday* which had been developed in a multimedia-rich context, for the sake of this study multimedia was deployed as a variable component between both styles. A series of eight sermons was preached, of which four were topically based and four followed a verse-by-verse expository style. Two of the sermons in each style had multimedia support and two did not. The subjects included 'Girl power', the Millennium and the End Times, food safety, abortion, divorce, Nelson Mandela, homosexuality, and Halloween.

Eighty volunteers were recruited from the congregation and an initial questionnaire enabled the sample to be allotted categories according to age, Christian commitment and church background. Participants undertook to fill out a brief questionnaire following the service each week. Questions were categorized as addressing issues of relevancy, growth, engagement, and clarity. The key question asked participants to award an overall rating for each sermon.

When the sermon series was complete an experienced researcher had follow-up interviews with twelve, randomly selected participants, three from each of the established age groups. The purpose of the interviews was to seek responses at the conclusion of the study and give an opportunity for additional comments and insights from the participants' reflections on their involvement in the study. All the research was carefully managed according to the strictest criteria to ensure the validity of the results.

It was expected that analysis of the results would show that younger people and those with a less 'churched' background, or lacking one completely, respond more positively to sermons in a topical style. A similar response was anticipated regarding the use of multimedia.

The corollary of this expectation was that with increasing age and level of exposure to church traditions, the response to the expository style would be more positive. Alongside this was anticipated a corresponding decrease in approval for the multimedia elements in the presentations.

## Results[16]

The level of data generated was colossal, with over 5000 pieces of information logged. In addition to this were the results from twelve follow-up interviews.

While it was disappointing that the results for the categories of Church Background and Christian Commitment were inconclusive, the results according to age groups were very interesting indeed. The key findings are as follows:

### i) Younger People Prefer a Topical Style

As expected, the results indicated clearly that, according to age, the participants in the study responded more positively to topical preaching as age decreases and more positively to expository preaching as age increases. A pattern is clearly visible with the over 60 group most heavily favouring expository sermons and the under 30s most clearly preferring the topical style. The 31–45s had a clear, though not quite as strong preference for topical sermons, while the 46–60s slightly favoured the more traditional verse by verse exposition.

## ii) 'Growth' is More Significant Than 'Relevance'

One of the things which the information gathered from the question-naires enabled us to do was analyse the results, question by question, to see if there was any correlation between the participants' overall rating of a sermon and other responses that might contribute to account for that rating. Correlating these responses gives some clear indication into the rationale behind the preference of each age group.

- For the under 30s: sermons that aid spiritual growth and are engaging score best.
- For the 31–45s: the growth of knowledge and understanding category was most significant.
- For the 46–60s: both growth categories and being engaged proved determinative
- For the 61+s: personal relevance and spiritual growth were defining factors.

Across the board, where correlation was revealed, it is interesting to see the categories of Growth and Engagement consistently out-perform Relevance and Clarity.

## iii) Multimedia Does Not Affect Responses

Surprisingly there appears to be little evidence to suggest any preference either for or against multimedia. The presence/absence of multimedia provided no noticeable effect on the results of the week-by-week questionnaire. Indeed, positive and negative responses to these sermons are spread relatively evenly across the responses of each age group. It seems from our survey that the use of multimedia is far more acceptable across the board than was anticipated, even with older people. The fact that the over 60s have lived with TV and film for most of their lives has obviously had an effect.

## iv) All the Various Styles are Acceptable

It is interesting to note from the overall distribution of raw scores for the rating question that very few low scores were registered. Indeed, only 8% of the scores occurred in the lower half of the range. Furthermore, analysis of these responses suggests that there was no strong adverse reaction to any particular sermon or to any particular style by any of the age groups. The absence of a strong adverse reaction across the categories is an important observation. It would appear to indicate a positive acceptance to the various presentational styles and media used in the preaching for this research.

The results from the interviews need to be treated with some caution because of the limited size of the sample. However, some unanticipated and intriguing observations were made regarding memory retention.

## v) Topical Sermons Stick in the Memory Better

Interviewees scored the topical sermons slightly higher than was originally the case in the questionnaire responses, while the expository sermons fared far worse with scores reduced by around 25%. The consistency in the responses to the topical sermons seems to indicate that this style aids memory retention, especially when viewed alongside the decline in how people rated the expository category.

## vi) Multimedia is Remembered Longer

Sermons with multimedia scored far better (up almost a third) while those without video and computer graphics fell away dramatically (down almost 50%). The overall improvement in the rating of multimedia-supported sermons suggests that this approach potentially aids memory retention to a significant extent. While there may be a measure of novelty that makes such sermons more memorable, the effect is quite marked and there is little evidence of novelty in the original responses. Anecdotal evidence also points to how 'quickly' the morning sermon passed, and how powerful some of the video images were.

## vii) Multimedia is a Significant Evangelistic Tool Alongside Relevant Communication

One of the standard questions asked each of the interviewees was, 'If you were to invite someone younger than yourself to West Croydon Baptist Church, who had no experience of church, which of the sermons would you prefer them to hear? Why?' All eight sermons were mentioned because they were relevant to those outside of the faith. However, the top four all had multimedia support. Certainly this group of people saw multimedia as a significant evangelistic tool even if their personal responses did not register the fact.

## Conclusions

In our individualistic and consumer-oriented culture it is accepted as self-evident that a pulpit style which begins with the life experience and questions of sermon listeners, such as topical preaching, will be far more effective than traditional expository preaching. The question that needed to be asked was, did this received wisdom bear scrutiny?

As far as West Croydon Baptist Church was concerned the answer is tantalizingly, yes and no. There are indications of some measure of truth in the observed trends that were discernible, yet they were not as clear-cut and self-evident as one would have expected. Neither was the introduction of multimedia and a new style viewed as such a dramatically different form as our vanity would perhaps have liked to have seen them to be. Even most over-60s quite liked watching video in church. Yet perhaps the most encouraging outcome to note as a pastor is that the most significant elements in a congregation's appreciation of a sermon appear to be issues of growth rather than issues of relevance.

*Most over-60s quite liked watching video in church*

But, at the end of the day, whatever style we feel led by the Spirit to adopt, the most important thing is that we are led by the Spirit. Whatever multimedia enhancements we make to our presentations and however informed we are by the latest insights of communication theory, the bottom line is that there is a foolishness about preaching in which God delights to do his work.

C H Spurgeon, the great Baptist preacher of the nineteenth century, recounts that it was among a despised people in an insignificant chapel of a peculiar sect that

> …the preacher read that precious text:— 'Look unto me, and be ye saved, all the ends of the earth; for I am God, and beside me there is none else'; and as I thought, fixing his eyes on me, before he began to preach to others, he said: 'Young man! look! look! look!'

And so the great preacher came to faith. We do well to remember that, in all our attempts to get the Word out effectively to our generation, there is another dimension. As Paul said,

> God was pleased through the foolishness of what was preached to save those who believe.                    1 Corinthians 1.21

# New Challenges

5

*What is it about tears? Sometimes they speak so much more clearly than any words we can say. And she could not find the words at all.*

We had prayed together and she just sat there beaming the most glorious of smiles with tear tracks running down her cheeks. It was the first time that Sabrina had been to church since she was christened. Now aged 20 she had walked in to our *First Sunday* event, and a presentation that looked at the person we aspire to be alongside the person we know we are—*'Love is…Me and me alone together'* was the subject. The Lord had profoundly touched her life and, there and then, she asked Jesus into her heart. As she repeated the words of a prayer after me, praying was such a new experience to her that she did not even know to close her eyes (I was peeking!).

When we began to think about this project it was only a dream, but dreams can come true. The church was neither particularly large nor particularly wealthy. Yet as the Lord led us down this path we found that he provided both the people and the resources we needed, when we needed them.

So what are some of the things we discovered on this journey into a very different way of doing evangelism?

## New Skills in Preaching

I guess we are all most comfortable with the things we know. When it comes to Baptists and sermons, expository and preaching go together as obviously as the bread and wine at Communion. Yet taking a Bible passage and systematically working through it is not the most helpful approach to attract, interest and hold the attention of those who are not yet Christians and are not therefore committed to Scripture. However, changing to a topical approach while remaining faithful to biblical truth requires learning a new and demanding discipline.

*The sermon becomes more of an overheard conversation, and we are all pretty nosy*

In the presentations we made we sometimes began with the life of an individual and used that as a starting point following the Willow Creek idea and asking what Jesus would say to them. The sermon becomes more of an over-heard conversation and, let us face it, we are all pretty nosy at heart! Prepa-ration then begins with thoroughly researching the individual's life. Bill Clinton and the Spice Girls were a little easier than James Bond and Barbie but Wesley Owen do not carry much stock on any of them! Added to which, these were not subjects that figured highly among my books either. Other times we have picked up on issues like health, *'Viagra, Jane Fonda, Trainspotting and Mr Blobby—what's that all about?'* and materialism, *'It is all about the money!'* Each one has required researching unfamiliar subjects in new disciplines to discover appropriate resources.

In preaching we also wanted to move from a more traditional, declarative style to something more conversational. To do this it was suggested that I sit on a barstool. This has worked well and for me has really helped to release a different kind of feel in my preaching. Conversely, others find it to be quite constricting and prefer to wander about to enable the same effect, albeit with not a lectern in sight!

Along with the conversational approach comes a more inductive methodol-ogy. That is, the talk is more of a journey. Hopefully it starts close to people's personal experience and then it invites them to come along to see where we end up. The points made are more implicit and listeners make their own connections. The contrast is really quite marked with the more traditional deductive preaching that spells things out more clearly and systematically.

Using video clips, computer graphics, audio files, dramatic reading and other media during a talk has a downside as well as an upside. The upside is pretty obvious, the downside for me is the script. To have other people making a contribution during the talk means that they have to know exactly where I am so as not to miss their cue. That demands far greater discipline than is at first obvious. Straying from what you have prepared can be disastrous.

*Straying from what you have prepared can be disastrous*

One other observation from our experience concerns spotlights. We looked to model our presentations on theatre and cinema. A darkened church also enhances the video screen projection of clips and graphics, so we did most of our work under spotlights. The disaster for a preacher is that you can no longer en-gage people's eyes as you preach. Yet I have found myself looking where I knew the eyes to be as I have attempted to establish that rapport with the audience. I am reminded of the observation by preaching guru Haddon Robinson who maintained that successful preaching always establishes inti-macy, even where intimacy would be thought to be impossible.

## A New Way of Preparing

I began preaching in 1976 and preparation has always been a solitary time of preacher, prayer, Bible and commentaries. It was completely novel for me to be part of a team preparing each presentation. Two months from the event we set the title and did the initial brainstorming. One month ahead we established potential issues, approaches and illustrative material. Then, two days after it was all over, we did a thorough debrief of what worked, what did not, and why! I love the approach with its teamwork, creativity and camaraderie, but it is not the most comfortable place for a preacher's ego. 'Faithful are the wounds of a friend,' but they are not painless.

*Teamwork is not the most comfortable place for the preacher's ego*

Of course, the technical involvement means a rehearsal. The video operator needs to know when the clips begin, when they end and where in the script they come. Precision is vital. The computer boffin may have loads of ideas of what to use to illustrate the talk, but to do that he needs the talk. Late Saturday night is no longer an option. If I am not to stretch pastoral relationships to breaking point, then the script must be ready a week in advance, save for final tweaking.

Encouragingly, we found that we had more people with technical expertise than we anticipated and, to our surprise, some who had previously sat very much on the fringe of the church's life were very willing to commit to this aspect of the ministry.

## A New Set of Resources

A new set of resources is required to pull off events like this. Our planning group had an indispensable role in advising and assisting in the preparation of talks. We could not have done without them! In addition, the Internet is invaluable. Search engines can give leads on where to find vital information.

As for more general resources, the Willow Creek Association and the Reaching the Unchurched Network are both worth joining. They run conferences, compile databases of resources and are an invaluable support network for any church wanting to travel down this road.

Willow Creek Assoc–UK, PO Box 622, Maidenhead, SL6 0YX
www.willowcreek.org

Reaching the Unchurched Network, PO Box 387, Aylesbury, HP21 8WH
www.run.org.uk

Some specific books that are worth a look include:

> *Cracking the Church Cocoon*, Mandy Watsham and Nicki Matthews (BRF). Explores creative evangelism through the performing arts.
>
> *Starting a Seeker Sensitive Service*, Ed Dobson (Zondervan).
>
> *Handbook of Contemporary Preaching*, Michael Duduit (ed) (Broadman Press). A good starter for exploring different preaching styles in bite-sized chunks.
>
> *Picking Up The Pieces: Can Evangelicals Adapt to Contemporary Culture?* David Hilborn (Hodder & Stoughton). This is a more serious read about wider issues.

## New Technology

This can be quite intimidating. Many churches are investing in the purchase of a video/data projector and there are few church offices that do not have their own computer now. These are fantastic resources, but the absence of finance need not deter you. While a top-of-the-range set of kit including projector, computer, software, VCR, vision mixer etc can take the shine off £10,000 it need not be so. Why not get three or four old TVs and wire them together with some leads from Tandy? Likewise, you do not need to have the latest all singing, all dancing computer. An old computer that someone wants to get rid of may well service your needs. And for software, you may find you already have Microsoft PowerPoint because the church office is using MS Office. If not there are other, much cheaper products that do a similar job: try Star Office for example. Be sure to ask if anyone has experience with these things and is prepared to help. You may be surprised.

## Copyright

This is one of the big issues that everyone wants to know the answer to regarding the resources we use. There is widespread confusion and differing advice that is proffered. No church wants to break the law in these matters; holiness is as important today as it has ever been. But there is no easy, centrally-administered scheme to join as is the case with other worship resources.

This is what we have discovered so far, but it may be subject to further clarification, alteration or change.

- Performing Rights Society licences (PRS), only cover music.
- Writing off for permission to the copyright holder for every video clip you use is fruitless, as it is not worth their time and expense to write back to you!

- Many companies operate on verbal consent if there is no charge for the event and you are a non-profit making organization.
- Educational institutions are often copyright exempt and it may be that some events could be classed as 'adult education.'

The copyright law is there to protect the artists, filmmakers and production companies. Many churches therefore endeavour to purchase a copy of any video they use so that the appropriate amount of money goes to the appropriate places. As the video clips can have a promotional value for the product, this may offer a workable way forward, with integrity.

## Other Stuff

Here is some other points that we have learned along the way:

- The unchurched do not necessarily think the way we do! We wanted a 'strap line' to go with the title *First Tuesday* for the cinema campaign and our advertising hoarding. We came up with what we thought were some brilliant ideas like '...*spiritual reality for the third millennium*' and '*help on your faith journey.*' When we tested them out on the general public, they invariably chose the line we thought was the weakest and had just included to make up the number, '*Christianity without being religious!*'

- These events are people, time and resources 'hungry.' Months come round very quickly and the creative energy needed to stay fresh in presentation, ideas, and video clips is very demanding. The creativity of the planning team regularly needs refreshing with new team members. A team will draw on what it knows, and what it knows is by and large governed by what it likes. Channel 4's *Friends* and *Ally McBeal* series may be a good source of relevant material, but you can only use it so much! A team drawn from your target 'social group' is therefore essential.

- Teamwork is essential. From front of house to the people who served refreshments we had between 20 and 30 involved each time.

- The clips say something about us, as they reflect our choice. For example, there is a difference between what we called by shorthand, 'laddish' and 'girlie' clips. All-action movies might look good if you are hooked on Bond, but what about romance, costume dramas and more inter-relational material? And because we were a multi-cultural church we quickly became aware of how 'white' much of our material was. Without that insight we would have been ignorant of our lack of cultural balance, and been inappropriately exclusive in our approach.

- Quality does not determine how many people come. After the first few events, expectations of an attendance explosion were high because of how well the events had been received by both members and visitors. Even one of the *London Today* TV crew commended us in glowing terms for the 'broadcast quality' of our presentation. Yet at times the numbers attending were disappointing. Only members of the congregation who are committed to bringing their friends, family and colleagues will actually bring people in to an event. While some did, most did not. Cold contact advertising might bring in one or two, but it will not fill a hall.

All this experimenting with different preaching styles, patterns of preparation and multimedia resources is a means to an end—communicating the gospel. On the day that Sabrina's encounter with the Lord unlocked tears of joy, in another part of the church sat David. He had worshipped with us twice before and had previously sampled Anglican and New Church services. A thirty-something professional convinced that there was more to life than success in marketing, he was hungry for spiritual reality. Talking to my colleague Joe Davis, who had spoken that morning, he said, *'I just had to keep pinching myself throughout the service today, it is just the most relevant event I have ever been to!'*

Dreams can come true, gospel preaching and contemporary culture can come together in the power of the Spirit. And in heaven, they rejoice!

# Notes

1 Laurence Singlehurst, *Sowing, Reaping, Keeping* (Leicester: Crossway, 1995) p 35.
2 Peter Brierley, *UK Christian Handbook* (London: Harper Collins, 1999) pp 0.3–0.4.
3 Neil Postman, *Amusing Ourselves to Death* (New York: Penguin, 1985) pp 16, 78 and 87.
4 Wade Clark Roof, *A Generation of Seekers* (New York: Harper Collins, 1993) pp 53–54 and 261.
5 George Barna, *Re-churching the Unchurched* (Ventura: Issachar Resources, 2000) pp 14–15.
6 Graham Cray, *Youth Congregations and the Emerging Church* (Grove Evangelism booklet Ev 57) p 12.
7 David Bosch, *Transforming Mission: Paradigm Shifts in Theology of Mission* (Maryknoll: Orbis, 1996) p 57.
8 John F Macarthur, *Ashamed of the Gospel: When the Church becomes like the World* (Wheaton: Crossway Books, 2001).
9 David Wells, *No Place for Truth* (Grand Rapids: Eerdmans, 1994) pp 96, 181, 215.
10 Os Guinness, *Fit Bodies, Fat Minds* (Grand Rapids: Baker, 1994) pp 10–11.
11 *ibid*, p 100.
12 Os Guinness and John Seels (eds), *No God but God* (Chicago: Moody, 1992) pp 23–33.
13 Richard Mouw, *Consulting the Faithful* (Grand Rapids: Eerdmans, 1994) pp 6, 13.
14 *ibid*, p 3.
15 *ibid*, p 5.
16 For a full digest of the research and results please contact the author by email on roger.standing@virgin.net.